Women! What's In Your Purse?

Taking Inventory of the Inner Me

Foreword

I will share with you in this book tips, experiences, and tools on how to be a more better you. This story will give you a sense of motivation and self esteem. It will help you to face challenges in which you face with force and focus.

Chapter One

The Inner Me

Several weeks ago I posted a blog on several social platforms entitled "Women! What's in your Purse? The blog received over 5,800 views. So I wanted to take the blog a little further and a little deeper. Long ago, their were times in which I didn't like the thought of a purse, not alone of carrying one.

I didn't have a need to be bothered with one. Kind of "tom boyish" style huh? No, I always felt that they would get in the way. I love to go places and feel free without carrying excess baggage around. I remember trying to cram everything into my pockets. No thief is going to rob me right, because I don't have a purse.

But as I got older, I found out, hey these things are pretty neat. So I began to fall in love with these little "doo hickeys". Some were coach bags, designer pieces, and wallet sized purses.

Today I'm still not a huge fan on them, but I found a way to make them work for me. As I began to have more responsibilities in life, I knew they were going to play a key point in my future. Purses can conceal things such as your credit cards, mascara, bills that you will need to pay and much more.

So a few years ago I began a new pitch in life, all types of ides and entrepreneurial thoughts came to mind. So the story is actually about, it's not about what in your physical purse but what's in the purse we carry inside. What's in your purse?, what's in your passion?, your dreams?, your DNA?, your career life, your goals, your accomplishments, what you have achieved, where do you see yourself in the next year?

So many times we plan and set goals far out such as five and ten years down the road. I couldn't respond about where I would be in the next five to ten years, because technology is rapidly changing and new initiatives are in the move so vastly that by the time you reach your five year goals, life will have advanced twenty times more.

My purse contains essentials in which I can provide more to my businesses, my clients, my networking circle, and it's not just local; it's global. Being a Ceo of two companies and show host of two radio hit shows, and the pastor of a church; it is imperative that I stay on the move for growth.

I want my purse to say more than what my business cards and websites can speak for me. At the start of our business, I was always scrambling for words to tell people about our vision and mission for the company.

Of course this will take time as you are growing towards your potential because your company is still in early development.

You may say, well I have had my business for about 5 years. It is still in development and will need nurturing continually. But the more I effectively worked on the business the mission became a reality to me and no longer had to think, scramble, or figure out what or who I was in the business, but I knew.

We as women must begin placing the right things into our purse. The business or career path that you are seeking may start off a little bumpy, but the more you work diligent towards your passions, the dreams and goals will become more evident that you are on the right path.

Changing some things in your purse will be essential for this process. I had to remove old patterns, old habits, small thinking, low self esteem, low worth value as a woman, family members whom were negative, friends whom were in my purse and needed to get out of there.

Surrounding yourself with strategic minded women will allow you to achieve the ultimate of success. Somehow other successful accomplishers will add much spice and growth to your inner purse and your outer purse(such as financially).

Do you not know that their are other women whom are out there that are waiting on you for them to coach, impact, and empower to grow you and your business.

So what's in my purse? Goal setting, more passion driven of my gifts and to impact women I possess, some patience,(not a lot, but some), more networking, greater audience, more professional venues, better communication, more effective planning, setting smaller goals, and not large ones to accomplish, and some critics.

Constructive criticism can sometimes play a positive role in your business. Just think about it! How would we really look or appear to the public and the nation if we never had anyone to tell us that we have made the coffee too black, or you need to change your venues, or your lighting is too dark in your meeting places?

We become angry at some criticism, but if they mean well , don't take it a second thought. Choke it up and swallow it. Sometimes our old wounds in life such as a bad divorce, a rocky relationship can cause women to become sour and take things the wrong way.

Women are accustomed to responding out of anger but it is really fear, but they have been wounded and trodden down in the past. This must leave our purse as well for potential and future success.

So what is not in my purse? Bad financial practices, the haters, negative feedback from those whom try to force you back because they have not accomplished anything, critic bloggers, (fear and the power to drive fear out of the door).

So the next time when you need an empowerment coach, first ask yourself, what's in my purse? Do I have the right tools in my thoughts to achieve this goal or project that I need to accomplish. You will be surprise at what you will find.

Lets Recap

Fill In the Blanks

What's In Your _____

Can Anxiety fit into My Purse?_____

True or False, Excessive spending habits are bad for business_____

Women are accustomed to responding out of_____

Are goal settings good for your purse?_____

Chapter Two

The Decisions In My Purse

What type of decisions are coming out of my purse? You know when I began in business, I made a lot of unhealthy choices and spent a lot of financial lucre(money). Some I regret and some I felt it was worth the pitch.

I had this passion of desiring to help others and my business began on a philanthropic level. I feel that women are givers and we always will be givers. It is our nature to do so.

Philanthropic is good for business just as long as you make the appropriate decisions and goals of how to manage it. You don't want your business to be in it's peak season where it can profit and you are still giving out excessively. There are many ways to give back to those whom desire it.

You can give back with free blogs, tutorials, webinars, and free conference settings. You must have a strategic plan as to how to plan your philanthropy. I spoke with a business colleague on last night and he is a giant in the marketing world. But he was so busy doing out of town events that he was needing to pick up where he left off in his own home town.

He called me and gave me his strategy of how he was going to do this. First he set up a free lunch and learn session for those whom desire to become an expert for blogging(financially) and then he connected and joined a local Business firm as a volunteer to help those whom were struggling in their business and to show them how to get clientele.

He came back to his own town and gave himself back to his own people by donating himself to them. In terms of "How can I help you?, What do you need from me to grow? I thought this was very cool.

Making the appropriate decisions can help steer you in the right path for success. Now what do you think could have happened if he had spent all of that time out of town helping others and he came back to our area and began charging people up to $500.00 for his session after he had been out of the game for a while in this area? This is usually his fee for assisting others in seminars and conferences.

I'm glad you asked. He would have experienced the shock of his life. In order for you to get you must first learn how to give and this comes with making the right decisions for your future and business.

He came in with the right strategic thought process to get his name and brand back into motion where he left off. People love when it's free right! So what better way for him to get back in the groove by giving himself to the people. His expertise were and will be accepted.

Do financial decisions play a role in my purse? Of course it does. Let's share a story with you. Melissa just opened a business called "Seeds 2 Business." She sees that her friend Martha has been in business for about two years and have purchased a new van.

Martha has clients and members in her business to foot the bill of her expense because she has membership fees in which she accrues from her paid members. Melissa sees this and now she desires to purchase her a van for her new flower shop. Martha has about 45 clients and

Melissa has seven. Would it be wise for Melissa to purchase a van and only have seven clients?

No! Melissa can carry those flowers in the back seat and the trunk of her car until she build her clientele enough for revenue in order to purchase a van. Sometimes we as women(including myself) have seen other women prosper in many areas. We like the glamour life and fame that they possess in their business.

So the first thing we think is that "We also have what it takes as the next woman." That may be true, but in do time though. Social media is one platform that keeps me moving because I see other women in successful positions and they are fired up for the job.

But one thing that I have learned is to make sure that I'm making good financial decisions in order for me and my household to stay above ground level. See we don't know what it took for Martha to get where she is today.

Or we don't know what it took for your colleague to be at that six figure job. Some women had to scratch and scuffle and all the while they were and are trying to build a business.

Some women suffered illnesses but they survived, they suffered divorce, but they survived through all of that, they suffered the lost of a job in order to build their own brand for themselves, they had to suffer their insignificant other walking out on them in order for them to take a stand for their dignity and character, the loss of a child in order to build a foundation for the name of the child while the grievance was taking place. We as women face challenges while making a buck for the table and chairs at home. I'm going to get a little religious here.

No matter what the devil set up for your bad, God will always turn it around and make something good out of it. In Genesis 90:20 it states "But as for you, ye thought evil against me; but God meant it unto good, to bring to pass, as it is this day, to save much people alive. So your passion and purpose in life is making a strong determination for others to follow

So the next time that you are visualizing someone else's portfolio, just think about what it may have taken for them to achieve that level. You only can do you for the moment.

Lets Recap

Did Melissa make the right decision in purchasing a new van?_____

How has the lesson changed your thinking_____

Why was Melissa so eager to purchase a new van?_____

Can we mimic others in their business?_____

Women Can You Carry My Purse?

Now that we have identified what's' in our purse. Let's pose the question: Can you carry my purse? Meaning can you handle what the next entrepreneur can deal with. I shared with you in the previous chapter about Melissa whom was trying to live the life of her friend Martha, but didn't have the financial support to do so. This brings the next topic in to clear view. Can you carry my purse? Who's purse are your trying to carry?

As I stated before, at the start of our business, I was always looking in someone else's' view mirror and did not see my own potential. Also we don't know what it took for the next woman to get to the level that she now holds and possess. Some women will work a lifetime for other bosses and entrepreneurs but will allow their own potential and dreams to die(emotionally). See there are many kinds of death. We can die spiritually, physically, mentally, and emotionally. You need a brand for your children to pick up and carry for upcoming future decisions. Why would I take my sons to a job interview when I can train them the business that I now own and operate.

This is why women hold their gifts and talents dear to them because they had to go through some pain in order to possess it.

I have heard other women say that "Oh she doesn't like to help people." Well the other woman may have a desire to help you but make sure that your motives are genuine before approaching that woman for help. I had a particular individual(woman) whom contacted me and she sound vibrant and happy.

I allowed her to make her pitch first in order to see what strategy she was trying to use. Well after she shared a lot of her personal business and I became comfortable; the truth came out. She was only interested in an exposure pitch through my business.

This places a bad taste in my purse when women or men, for that fact, will get you all hyped up and you think you are about to do business. But in fact they are looking to get something from you for nothing. These are the people in your purses that you don't want to carry around with you.

Everyone can't handle the life or business challenges that you or I had to encounter. So let's explain this a little deeper. Janet desires to make the seven digits for her business.

She has not trained herself through networking, seminars, webinars, or any tutorials on how to build a relationship with other women. she doesn't know and isn't aware that it takes building an audience and brand with others in order to achieve success in anything.

So she is invited to this gala and they are awarding one of her friend colleagues in her business. Jane says to herself "OOOHHH look what she has. Jane begins to plan a way to make her company grow to achieve that dollar figure.

She doesn't have a financial goal nor a budget. She hires people with low skills and knowledge of the business, she purchases things that she will not need until she begins to grow; all due to what someone else has.

The next quarter her sales report comes out and she has plunged in the four digits in her business and now she is frustrated due to her visualizing someone else's success, which was probably built years ago before she came into business.

I'm not in the business to carry your purse (meaning your dreams, your vision, your goals, your passions) I was strategically made and developed to carry what I place on the inside of my purse. This is why so many women error.

They are looking, biting, and chewing off someone else's success. Make a decision today that no matter what someone else is accomplishing that you can achieve as well in due time.

It takes time to build a village. Women create businesses to build villages and territories not just monuments. Get up from there and make your own P-U-R-S-E.

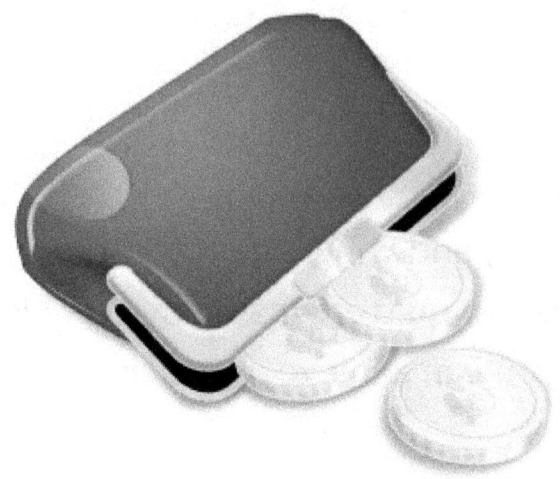

Let's Recap

Fill In the Blanks

Can You Carry My _____?

What should have Jane done?_____

Is success built overnight?_____

True or False Jane is a spender?_____

Do I keep focused on others or my own business?_____

How can I assist other women?_____

About The Author

Mrs. Diane Winbush is the Author of "Making Cents"(A Child curriculum) "The Seven Steps to a Fall of A Clergy," "The Life of a Prophet & Prophetess." She is the radio show host & producer of "Women Who Rock With Success & "The Professional Pastors Broadcast." Mrs. Winbush is Prophetess & Senior Pastor of Saint Petersburg Global Ministries, Chief Executive Officer of "The Networking Partners & "The National Extraordinary Professional Women & My Princess Teens Ministry." She is also the wife of Clifford Winbush, a mother of four sons and seven grandchildren. These businesses and ministries can be contacted at info@extraordinarywomens.com.

www.ingramcontent.com/pod-product-compliance
Lightning Source LLC
Chambersburg PA
CBHW081819170526
45167CB00008B/3465